TERESA A. STITH

LIVE LIKE YOU KNOW

Embracing Our Freedom in Christ

LIVE LIKE YOU KNOW

Copyright © 2019 Teresa A. Stith

All rights reserved. This book is protected by the copyright laws of the United States of America. This book may not be copied or reprinted for commercial gain or profit. The use of short quotations or occasional page copying for personal or group study is permitted and encouraged. Permission will be granted upon request.

Unless otherwise identified, scripture quotations are from the King James Version of the Bible. Copyright © 1982 by Thomas Nelson, Inc. Used by permission. All rights reserved.

Please note that certain pronouns referring to the Father, Son, and Holy Spirit may be capitalized to acknowledge God and any such titles referring to Him. Please note just the opposite when referring to satan. We choose not to capitalize his name or acknowledge him in any way, even to the point of violating grammatical rules.

ISBN-13: 978-1-7332744-9-4

ISBN-10: 1-7332744-9-9

Publisher- A Faith That Works Publishing

Website: afaiththatworks.com

LIVE LIKE YOU KNOW

Embracing Our Freedom In Christ

If the Son therefore shall
make you free
You shall be free indeed
(John 8:36)

DEDICATION

This book is dedicated solely to my Leaders who have exemplified over and over again the true character of Christ Jesus. I have watched them over the years stand firm under the harshest of circumstances daring to believe that God would show up, and with His righteous right hand give us the victory. I have watched them love on others unconditionally in unseemly unlovable situations. I have witnessed them stand boldly in the face of adversity and declare over and over again that God will provide.

In situations that have caused me to cry out to God in such deep agony, I have seen them hold fast to their faith and rejoice in the "faithfulness" of our God. Every challenge that they've faced, have all been met with extraordinary faith in the God who has proven Himself to be MORE THAN ENOUGH. My Leaders have taught me to "Live Like You Know" what God has said concerning your life. My Pastor says that

"God is an All- Sufficient God, and to endure this journey, we must be skilled in the area of waiting." We must wait in faith being steadfast, and unmovable. He has often asked "do you have the faith to believe that God can change your situation?" If so, then live like you know He will! We must not allow the enemy to use our situations and circumstances to oppress us, because surely we can rejoice right now!

> Rejoice in the Lord always:
> and again I say, Rejoice.
> Let your moderation be known unto all men
> the Lord is at hand.
> (Philippians 4: 4, 5)

You have earned your right to DANCE…so DANCE!

INTRODUCTION

When I began working on this book, my intentions were to let people know *my* perspective on being able to *enjoy* freedom in Christ. For years I was stuck in a place as a Christian where I was not really sure about all that I could do as a child of God. Of course, I had made good Christian friends over the years and had developed good Christian relationships but I felt that there was still something missing. I felt like I was still not free to live like I wanted to. I felt like I was always being bombarded with some kind of rule "don't do this" or "you can't do that" but never having the power or the freedom to exercise my own rights. I was silent though, over the years as I watched and observed others while I learned about the Lord. I could not seem to get this thing right! I would go to church, I would hear the word preached, I knew what the word was telling me to do, but time and time again, I stumbled and fell back into my old way of living. Living for the Lord became such a battle for me that I eventually turned back to the world. Now it wasn't because of anything that God did, but my own limited understanding as to how to live a life of freedom in Christ Jesus. My own thoughts drove me to make bad decisions but of course, when the world beat me down as far as I would allow it to, I came running back to God to fix my life all over again. This cycle would go on and on like a revolving door until I decided that I would listen to God and do things His way, rather than trying to make Him change His word to fit my unstable lifestyle.

    Now that I am rooted and grounded in the word of God, I understand that when I accepted Christ into my life, I gave up all control over my life to Him. I gave Him permission to do with my life as He saw fit and I agreed that "my will" would have no part in the decisions that He made concerning me. Afterall, I wanted God's will to be perfected in me. So I understand also that I don't have a life because His life is being lived through me. I do not regret having trusted God with my life because He is certainly doing a better job than I ever could bringing structure, order, and substance to it. As a matter of fact, Jesus is the best thing that ever happened to me. We error on this journey not knowing the truth of God's word and lacking the understanding that we need to serve the Lord with our whole hearts. Understand this, freedom in Christ begins with the freedom of our minds. If you can't be free in your thinking, you won't be free in your body because the way you think will ultimately determine how you will behave! I'll say again:

If the Son therefore shall make you free, you shall be free indeed (John 8:36).

When we accepted Christ into our lives, every sin that we committed up to that point, and those that we will ever commit in the future has been forgiven. Should that be a green light to sin? God forbid! In essence, I felt like I could not live like I wanted to because there was still something in me that wanted to do what "Teresa" wanted to do. The flesh still wanted to sin, and I had no control over that feeling without Christ. I wanted to blame everyone else and I wanted to be upset with everyone else including those in the church, all because my intentions were wrong! The church however, was not backing down from what they knew and believed, simply because I had an issue with it! So I had to eventually pull my own thinking up until it matched what the word of God said. I had not understood how to separate myself from my sin and I was upset with the church folk because every time I went, there was another word that convicted me of my wrongdoing. They challenged me to change my sinful ways and truth be told, I didn't want to. I often wondered how all of those people lived their lives without sin and was happy about it (laugh out loud). I loved sin, especially since I did not know that I wasn't supposed to! I thank God for the blood of Jesus that covered me in my ignorance, but I struggled in learning to live life without sin and still have joy! Have you ever sit in church and it seemed that everything that the Pastor said was about you? I tell you what, I went through it! It seemed like every message, every Sunday was about something that I knew that I was guilty of doing. I sit there shaking my legs, twittling my thumbs, and even saying Amen at times, knowing full well what I had just did the night before! There were times that I wanted to get up and run out of the church because the Word was convicting me so strongly, but I sit there under it because I was too ashamed to move. I tell you the truth, God knows how to put the fire underneath us, especially when He is calling you to a *changed* life. I truly owe Him my life, but I had to go through this process. Listen, if you are someone whose always finding something wrong at church, it's not the *thing* that's wrong…IT"S YOU! God is taking you through a process of change, and it can be rather frustrating when you lack the understanding of what is actually taking place. Not only that, because you cannot control what is happening in the Spiritual realm, your flesh wants to fight back. I had to learn that I could not do *what I wanted to do* anymore because I was not the same person anymore. I could not do what I wanted to do as a child of God and expect Him to be pleased with my choices. God does not conduct Himself unseemingly in any situation, and if His Spirit is truly living and at work in us, we won't behave foolishly either because…**The love of God will constrain us.**

Either way, **Christ's love controls us.**
Since we believe that Christ died for all,
we also believe that **we have all died to our old life**
(2 Corinthians 5:14) -New Living Translation

This is not to say however, that there will not be some issues that may arise in some churches, but keeping our focus on Christ will not only show us how to respond when these situations occur, but it will help us to keep God's love as the motivating factor when we are communicating with others in the faith. We can truly live like we know when we can do like Mary did and choose that "*good part*" to be our guide. Think about it….read this:

So we come to a scene in Luke chapter 10 (paraphrasing) where Martha invites Jesus into her home. Martha had a sister called Mary, who was seated at Jesus' feet and heard his word. Martha was distracted by all the preparations that she had to make and asked Jesus "Lord don't you care that my sister has left me to do the work alone? Tell her to help me!" Jesus responds and tells Martha that she is worried about many things, but the thing that is needful, **Mary has chosen** to partake of, and that will not be taken away from her (Luke 10:38-42).

In "living like you know" you have to decide what will benefit you and what will not. The word of God makes it easy for us to know *how* we should choose. It is my hope that you will discover something in this book that will move you from where you are to where you have longed to be for years. "Living like you know" doesn't have to be a figment of your imagination, you can actually have what you say by simply transforming your mind to believe that:

1. God wants to give you His best
2. It is obtainable despite your current situation
3. You qualify simply because God says you do
4. You are already equipped for greater

5. It is time!

Lose the fear! Fear keeps you stagnant and fear is deceiving. Fear tells you all of the reasons why you are incapable of achieving the thing that you've desired for so long. Fear is not your friend nor your safe haven, it is another ploy of the enemy to keep you from birthing out your purpose to the world. Overcome fear by daring to step out and embrace life by "Living Like You Know" that this is what you were called to do and do it with GRACE.

> What a wonderful world this would be, it would
> If only we'd learn how to see the good
> Oh how rich our lives would be
> If we changed the way we chose to see
> How pleasant and grand a time we'd have
> If we gave Christ our hearts and left them there.
> Living like you know you're free in Christ
> Is only a fragment of our God-given right
> Embrace the love that He wants to give
> Which only perfects the way we live
> My God truly wants to give you His best

But you have to learn how to pass His test
Be open to what the Spirit shares
Because He will always make you aware
The time we have on this side is short
But surely enough time to make a choice
Don't let your works be done in vain
True worshippers seek to praise His name

And God *seeketh such* to worship Him.

LIVE LIKE YOU KNOW

TABLE OF CONTENTS

Chapter 1: Get Free Stay Free………………………..1

Chapter 2: Christian Sense vs. Common Sense……15

Chapter 3: Recalling What God Has Said…………..23

Chapter 4: Childlike Faith…………………………29

The Recap: Live Like You Know…………………..37

Bonus: Living Life on Purpose……..……………....43

About The Author………………………………….47

CHAPTER ONE

GET FREE
STAY FREE

When God frees you from a situation or circumstance, it is entirely up to you to stay free. The entire process of staying free involves refusing to be entangled again with those things that once had you bound. I will give you some examples. In my first book "A Faith That Works" I share with you how I isolated myself from other people primarily because of something that was wrong in me. I felt unloved, rejected, and a host of other emotions that ultimately resulted from the way that I looked at situations and circumstances. When you are in a place of defeat or a state of depression, what may seem real to you may not actually be real in real life. It only seems to be real to you because of the place that you are in (in your mind). I grew up feeling that I was unloved by certain people and I spent the majority of my life in this lonely place surrounded by feelings and thoughts of rejection. It would take years for me to get up the nerve to confront what I felt. I learned that it had all been a trick of the enemy to keep me bound in my mind and stagnate in my growth in the Lord. After talking with these people and realizing that they loved me without conditions, I could finally move forward to a place of freedom in Christ. But look at the time that was lost! I had literally allowed situations and circumstances to beat me down to the point of not wanting to pull myself out of the mess. I found it easy though, to place the blame on someone else rather than accepting the fact that I had isolated my own self from what was actually real because of what I thought I was seeing in my mind. We know that the mind is a terrible thing to waste, and until you understand where the battle begins, you will keep fighting with carnal weapons, and you will keep losing every time! YOU MUST take control over your thinking. I can tell you this now, but back then I allowed the negative things that others would say push me further into a state of depression. I was not able to comprehend that I had the power to fight against the thoughts that often bombarded my mind. But rather than fight, I found it easier to dwell on these thoughts not realizing the impact that they were having on me mentally. I thought that I was satisfying that place in me that wanted justification to feel bitter, but I was only setting myself up to lose miserably. Suicidal thoughts began to take root. For the suicidal person, this is not a game. It is actually one of the most dangerous and vulnerable places that a soul could dwell. In this place, the individual hangs on to a mere thread between life and death and the will to die is overwhelmingly greater than that to live, but you must hang on to God's word. I was still in the process of learning God when I found myself in this place. If you ever find yourself in this place and you don't know God, you better hope against hope! What I mean is that God is nearer to us than what we believe and He knows when we truly desire Him to step into our situation and bring restoration to our lives. When I found myself in this place, I kept hanging on to the word that my Pastor consistently poured into me until I was able to lift myself out of my mess. I'm so grateful during this time in my life that I had a Pastor who literally walked me through the process of healing. He stayed in constant contact with me and he visited me often. My Pastor ministered faith to me and gave me hope that began to build me up in my Spirit. They say that God puts people in your life for a reason, and my Pastor was truly my angel to guide me throughout this phase in my life. The reality was though, that when he left, I had to battle my thoughts all over again. Thinking on my situation only put me right back to where I thought I had been delivered from. I was so tired of struggling. I had four kids that I had to provide for and it became rather overwhelming to the point that I began to have thoughts of doing something illegal to free myself from this trouble. Have you ever felt that you were so hard pressed to make ends meet, that you actually began to consider doing something that you would never do, if you were thinking right? My thinking was the issue, and because I was thinking wrong, the wrong behavior began to grip my life. I did not have the finances or the resources that I needed to get ahead and I found myself moving from one place to the next because I could not pay rent consistently. I did not have a car because I could not afford one and I had to rely on other people to get me from one place to the other. Let me tell you, when you are struggling, people will isolate themselves from you. They are so afraid that you will ask them for help and they know that they don't really want to help you so, rather than just tell you that they don't want to help, they try to avoid you at all costs. These are some of the same people who sit in the church and boldly profess how they love everybody. "I love the Lord", they say.

    Now this is not a hit below the belt towards the church. This was actually God showing me at this time, who was who when it came to those who named the name of Christ, and the condition that our hearts should be in when others come to us for help or just in general. Our first mind should not be that "they just want something from us" our first mind should be "what can I give?" or "how can I assist?" Remember, we have the words of Jesus embedded in our hearts and we should be ready to share what we have with whomever the Lord may send our way. The word tells us that MANY will come in that day saying "Lord, Lord, did we not prophesy in your name, and cast out demons in your name, and do many mighty works in your name?" And then I will declare to them, "I never knew you; depart from me, you workers of lawlessness." (Matthew 7: 22-23). We must not rejoice only at hearing God's words, but in putting into practice those things that have been spoken by Him.

People were not all that willing to help me. In their minds, I had brought all of these unfortunate events on myself and rightly so, but now I was looking for help to free myself from this way of living and I could not get people to see that I had truly changed. I began to realize that my battle was not with these people but between myself and my will, and where God was trying to take me. He was killing my flesh and I was acting out in my body the only way that I knew how, to bring relief to the chaos associated with the transformation that was taking place in me. Let me interject here and say that you do not have to be on drugs to become "dependent" or addicted to something. I was so addicted to needing other people's help that I became crippled. I could not seem to do anything for myself. I was prevented from gaining the confidence that I needed to move forward with my life due to my dependency. I had allowed myself to be trained only to see my troubles. I locked myself away from my children and the rest of the world and I lived daily with no hope. I turned to drugs. I have only shared this part of my life with a few people. I began to sell drugs as a means to fix my financial situation. I sold drugs to people that I would have never expected to be on drugs. They never expected that I would become so desperate that I would choose this route either, but it happened. Now I was not a Queen-pin or anything of the sort, but I did what I deemed necessary to survive at the time and it didn't even work.

I can recall one night taking a ride out to

Richmond, Virginia with some friends of mine trying to make some money in a neighborhood that I absolutely knew nothing about. My friends supposedly knew a little more about the drug game than I did. We sit outside in the car while one of my friends got out to make the transactions. As I sit in the car as pregnant as I could be, I somehow wished to God that I had just stayed home. What was I thinking? Oh, I'm here because I wasn't thinking! All kinds of thoughts began to cloud my mind and lo' and behold, I was not surprised when something began to go terribly wrong. I began to pray, "Lord, if you let me make it home, I promise that I will never come back here again." The guys that my friend was trying to sell drugs to begin to make a big fuss over the fact that they did not know him and he's in their neighborhood trying to sell drugs. I tell you, it was probably the longest night that I've had to endure, but when I made it back home, home is where I stayed. Still struggling, I chose to struggle rather than die trying to live. I gave up this way of life. My Pastor played a pivotal role in my life to help me to be able to stand on the Word of God and believe that God had an ultimate plan and purpose for my life although I could not see it. He kept coming and he kept speaking life into me until I was able to begin fighting my thoughts on my own. I had heard what my Pastor said about my life and how I was an overcomer. I remember him saying that the Greater One lived in me. He said that God had given me the power to tread over serpents and scorpions and over all the power of the enemy and that nothing shall by any means harm me (Luke 10:19). I was able to teach myself (through his teachings) how to apply the "Right Word" to actual situations based on what I had learned about the Lord. Life became easier as it began to make sense to me. Although my situations did not change immediately, I was able to look at them differently…with hope! When I begin to focus my thoughts and attention on the hope that I have in Christ, I was able to begin taking the steps needed to fix my life. See, hope moves you to take action! Hope gave me the will to live again and now that I was free, I had to maintain my own freedom. The battles in my mind against my own thoughts did not stop because I gained a little knowledge. They tried me even harder than before, but I stood my ground. What I learned during this time, was that whenever I applied the RIGHT WORD to these and other situations, I overcame and endured. I learned something about myself and my faith. When we learn to grow IN these moments, we will walk away with the knowledge, the skills, the awareness, and the wisdom to overcome future battles. When God frees you, it is your responsibility to stay free! God is not going to do it for you. He will give you everything that you need to fight the battle, but YOU have to be willing to use what He gives you to sustain yourself. You have to become consistent and persistent as the battle intensifies, because it will. You will be met with obstacles that will cause you to want to sink back into your hole, but you must fight. The word tells us to fight the good fight of faith (1 Tim. 6:12).

> No, I keep on disciplining my body, making it serve me so that after I have preached to others, I myself will not somehow be

disqualified (1 Cor. 9:27).

You may be overcome with grief due to a loss or some overwhelming situation. You may feel helpless and distraught. One thing after another may be constantly battling you and pushing you toward the edge, but I declare to you today that you are free in the name of Jesus! Be healed in your mind. Turn your face away from your problems and fix your eyes on Jesus! When God delivers you out of a situation, don't feel pressured to go back in. It is the enemy's job to make you feel obligated to that thing. He will tell you all the reasons why you should go back to it, but I promise you that there is abundance ahead of you. God knows it, and the enemy knows it too. He doesn't want you to enjoy what God has for you, he wants to keep you bound. He wants you to stay under his authority in the world. But you have to keep moving forward. I have gone back to broken and abusive relationships because I did not want to be alone. I have turned to the world many times because I did not want to wait on my deliverances. I felt like God was taking too long to answer so I stepped ahead of Him. I tell you the truth, the consequences that came from not waiting on God was not worth stepping out of His will at all.

I can recall in late 2015 while sitting in my living room reading the Bible in Romans chapter 6, how the Holy Ghost began to impress truth upon me. I had read this chapter so many times before, but here it is that on this day, the word became so much more alive to me. Here's the recap…

In verse 2 the word states: "God forbid. How shall we, that are dead to sin, live any longer therein?" This is simply implying that because Jesus bore our sins on the cross, when he died our sins died with him. **Verse 3** states (paraphrasing) "Don't you know that we who were baptized into Jesus Christ, were baptized into his death?" This means that when Christ died with our sins laid upon him, we were <u>right then</u> made free from sin…so **WE DO NOT HAVE TO SIN! Verse 4** states that (paraphrasing) "just like Christ was raised up from the dead by the glory of the Father, even so we also should **walk in newness of life." Verse 6** says **"KNOWING THIS"**

(Live Like You Know) that our old man is crucified with Him, that the body of sin might be destroyed, that henceforth **WE SHOULD NOT** serve sin." **Verse 7** states "For he that is dead is freed from sin."

Now...**LIVE LIKE YOU KNOW!** You do not have to do anything that is against the Word of God. The enemy will cause us to become so overwhelmed by life's circumstances that we feel like our only option is to return to the former things. We begin to make hasty decisions that often lead us into more trouble. Get free and stay free. Do not lower your standards because you cannot see how a way will be made. Stand firm on what God says and resist the temptations. You are not in this alone and if you learn to trust God, He will not fail you. I will tell you that I was miserable in a relationship that was very abusive and I wanted to leave, but I could not afford to take care of myself and my children without the help that this man provided (when he wanted to). If he did not want to help, he didn't help and I was foolish enough to put up with it because I did not think that I could survive on my own without him. What a lie the devil made me believe! Let me tell you, for every issue that you will ever face in life, there's a remedy for it in the Word of God. But YOU have to want to be free! Put your foot down and move yourself out and into that greater place that God has for you. Don't just settle for this, when you can have THAT too!

BE RELENTLESS

CHAPTER TWO

CHRISTIAN SENSE VS. COMMON SENSE

What may seem to be common sense to you, may not always be good Christian sense. Common sense is the ability to judge things, make sound decisions, and act in a reasonable way using your own intellect, skills, or training. Christian sense is the ability to judge things, make sound decisions, and act in a reasonable way according to the Spirit of God within you. I have learned to judge things by the word of God while trusting the Spirit of God within me. What does God say about it, or what would Jesus do in this situation? I think that life would be much easier if we learn to acknowledge God in all of our ways. As I stated earlier, some of the decisions that I made in life was not because I did not know better, but because I felt pressured to make a decision right away, and did not allow myself time to think things through. There is always a consequence behind your actions, but when put between a rock and a hard place, the consequences are not always considered and do not seem as severe. I only wanted what I thought I needed at the moment. My God, my God!

See, having good Christian sense teaches us how to put more focus on what God has said rather than what we think or feel. Our feelings and our thoughts have a tendency to lead us astray and take us off course. As human beings, we have a natural tendency to react or respond to trouble or unforeseen events. The way that we respond is usually with panic rather than patience, or with fear rather than faith. We run away from the Word of God when that should be the first thing that we run toward. I used to hear my Pastor say that we have become accustomed to living life backwards. We cry at funerals when we should be rejoicing (Especially if the person died having a relationship with the Lord). When you apply the word of God to your life and do it consistently, you will see things change dramatically. You will still be tried and tested of course, but the peace that comes with trusting God is priceless!

    I'm reminded of one of my sons who was learning how to trust in the Lord. No matter how much I would tell him to trust God to work things out for him, he would always go out on a rampage trying to figure things out on his own. I would be so frustrated in trying to get him to see what I already knew, but he had to learn God for himself. So I watched him fall down and get up, fall down and get up until he finally learned how to put God in what he was dealing with. We have access to God in a way that the world doesn't, but we won't call on Him… why? God tells us to call upon Him in the day of trouble and He will deliver us (Psalm 50:15) and we still won't do it. Oftentimes, we have to experience some hardship that drives us to our knees and cause us to remember that Christ died to give us access to the throne of God. The Lord urges us to come boldly to the throne of grace, that we may obtain mercy and find grace to help in our time of need (Hebrews 4:16).

It's Easier Done Than Said

We often like to say that it's easier said than done, but it's actually easier to just **do** what God has instructed. This is where the transforming of your mind comes into play. See, we have to **think** like

Christ in order to get results like Christ. Let this mind be in you which was also in Christ Jesus (Phil. 2:5). Repeat after me…**Lord, I believe you.**

In this season, we can't rely on what we think we know, we have to rely solely on the leading of the Spirit of God. If you're reading this book and don't know how to do that, pause for a moment and ask God to come into your heart and be Lord over your life. Confess Jesus with your mouth by saying "Lord I believe that You are the Son of God and I also believe that You died on the cross for my sins and rose on the third day with all power in Your hands. Now rejoice because you are saved! You cannot rightly discern Spiritual things if you do not have a relationship with the Lord and connected to Him by the Holy Spirit. When you are truly trusting God as your Source, your former way of thinking goes out the window. You

can't think like you used to because you don't have the same mind that you used to have. Of course it's the enemy's (satan's) job to convince you that nothing took place and you are still the same ole person you were, but you have to believe God's report, not satan's. Practicing good Christian sense helps us to recognize our own behavior, as well as gives us Spiritual awareness when we are not responding to situations and circumstances as we should being children of God. Make sure that even your practice of these things are genuine. Sometimes when we practice certain behaviors, they become more of a routine for us than a genuine need to change that behavior. This takes discipline. Paul said it this way in 2 Cor. 4:10 "Always bearing about in the body the dying of the Lord Jesus, that the life also of Jesus might be made manifest in our body." We all have heard how cattle and even slaves at one point in time were branded to show under whose ownership they belonged. They would have the markings of signs or symbols that identified them with their owners. This is what Paul is explaining here. Paul clearly states that he has all the markings in his body to show that he belongs to Christ. He says that he was "More" as a minister of Christ, in labours more abundant, in stripes above measure, in prisons more frequent, and in deaths often (2 Cor. 11:23). Paul says in 1 Cor. 9:17 NIV "I discipline my body like an athlete, training it to do what it should. Otherwise, I fear that after preaching to others I myself might be disqualified. God says if any of you lack wisdom, you should ask God, who gives generously to all without finding fault, and it will be given to you (James 1:5). God has even made it possible that we do not have to lift a finger to fight. We are commanded "Do not be afraid. Stand firm and you will see the deliverance the Lord will bring you today" (Exodus 14: 13).

As stated earlier, we have to not only be disciplined in our bodies, we must be conditioned in our minds to not allow our thoughts or emotions to interfere with God's purpose and plan for our lives. Using good Christian sense teaches us to rely on God and His word and WAIT for the manifestation of the promises of God for our lives. Let's look at how Solomon summed it up:

> "I have observed something else under the sun.
> The fastest runner doesn't always win the race,
> and the strongest warrior doesn't always win the
> battle. The wise sometimes go hungry,
> and the skillful are not necessarily wealthy.
> And those who are educated don't always lead
> successful lives. It is all decided by chance,
> by being in the right place
> at the right time"
>
> Ecclesiastes 9:11 (NIV)

CHAPTER THREE
RECALLING WHAT GOD HAS SAID

In order to "Live Like You Know" you must recall what God has said to you. Your obedience to God's instructions will determine your peace, your joy, and your happiness. You cannot recall what God has said to you if you do not practice keeping yourself in a position to hear. It's very hard to hear God if we are talking while He is talking. So how do you know when God is talking? The Holy Ghost (God's Spirit within us) is always leading us and guiding us, and correcting the error of our ways. Sometimes, God is silent, but only because He has already given us instructions. He waits patiently for us to follow the last thing He told us to do before He can move us along to the next step. When we get quiet before God, we are telling Him, "Lord, I am in position, I am ready to obey."

I had a coworker that was very good at irritating me. What irritated me about her was that whenever I would talk, she would talk too. I never had a chance to finish what I was saying because she always wanted to be heard. She was so adamant about getting what she wanted to say out, that she could not receive anything. Whenever I would offer a solution for her issues, she already had a solution. I tell you the truth, there were times when I wanted to walk politely over to her and put a piece of masking tape over her lips so that she could be quiet long enough to hear and receive instructions. Afterall, she did ask for my opinion! During some of our conversations, I would just stop talking to let her say everything that she wanted to say, and when she had finished and would ask "oh, what were you saying?" I would politely say, "nothing." I mean there were times that I really hoped that she would see her error in cutting me off, excuse herself, and allow me to finish, but she never did. This is how some of us are with God and as a result, experience has to be our teacher. We just yap, yap, yap away as God tries to teach and instruct us and because we do not listen, He sits silently and patiently by waiting for us to zip it so that He can move us forward. We have wondered why it has taken our prayers so long to be answered, and it is because we have not allowed ourselves to be still before the Lord to hear from Him. When we don't allow God to speak to us, He becomes silent and we become disoriented and frustrated because we don't know our next move. God is a perfect Gentleman and will not interfere with our choices. He only urges us to choose life, but He will never force us to. Don't worry, God is not upset with us when He is silent, but He uses it as a teachable moment. God will remain silent for so long that it will literally force us to listen for His voice. I'm a witness to that! God will become silent for so long that it begins to stretch you, pull you, and whip your heart into fellowship with Him! God will become silent for so long that it begins to press you down so low that you feel like you are dying. In this state of pressing, (I'm talking about a Spiritual press here) all hell is still breaking loose (physically) in every area of your life. Any and everything that could go wrong, does go wrong, and you feel like you are on the brink of a total mental breakdown. You will do one of two things…you will STAND up in it or you will quit! The battle is not designed for you to give up. God will use physical hardships and battles to bring about the Spiritual results we need that will get us into Heaven. The Bible states "Beloved, I wish above all things that thou mayest prosper and be in health, even as thy soul prospereth" (3 John 1:2). In silence, God is perfecting something in us that oftentimes we are not even aware of. Because we so desperately want to hear God's voice at this point, we learn to shut down everything around us and we become still.

    For I know the thoughts that I think toward you, saith the Lord, thoughts of peace, and not evil, to give you an expected end (Jeremiah 29:11). Paraphrasing…I believe that God is saying that when we set our hearts to seek Him, by recalling what He has said to us, THEN…He will attend to us! He will confirm His promises to restore us, and we will be able to go to Him through prayer and He will listen to us (Berean Study Bible). If God is silent, then we have work to do.

How Soon We Forget

In the book of Deuteronomy, Moses constantly reminds the people to not forget the words that were spoken to them by God. They were to not only remember, but to teach the word diligently to their children and talk of them when they sit in their houses. When they walked in the way, they were encouraged to speak of the word. When they laid down, and when they got up the next morning, the word should be on their hearts. Deuteronomy 6: 8 goes on to say that they should bind the word for a sign upon thine hand, and they shall be as frontlets between thine eyes. Thou shalt write them upon the posts of thy house, and on thy gates (Deuteronomy 6: 7-9). What God is telling us is to be clothed with the word. What He has instructed us and commanded us to do should always be before us. It is the first thing that we should see when we arise in the morning. It is all that we should be discussing to our children and to one another. We should not forget it! God has given us His divine guidelines to follow that we may experience true freedom in Christ, but we are in danger of forgetting these things and damaging our relationship with God when we go whoring after things in this world that appear to be more appealing. One thing about the Lord is that although you may forget what God has said, He never forgets what He told us to do. Our blessings follow obedience, while disobedience brings the withholding of blessings. Ask the Holy Ghost to bring back to your remembrance those instructions that God gave you. If you are sincere, God will redirect your steps and show you what to do. If you are not, then just like the Israelites, you will find yourself going around the same ole' mountains (situations and circumstances) and never getting to that land (those blessings) that God has already prepared and have stored up for you. He wants you to be free, BUT YOU must choose your freedom!

REMEMBER

CHAPTER FOUR
CHILD-LIKE FAITH

I absolutely adore my grandson KJ as I do all of my grandchildren, but I am particularly fond of him. I have watched him and studied his behavior from his first moments of life, and it has been the most amazing thing to see. His curiosity for the things that he sees and hears leaves an infectious smile on my face. He has grown to love the outdoors. Every car that drives by our house gets his full attention. He trusts so easily. As he learns his place in the midst of the chaos all around him, he chooses his own peace-playing with his toys. He is so particular about everything! He will not eat any kind of food. He is not big on candy or ice-cream like most kids. He is still going through a process of learning what is good for him and what is not. He may enjoy these things as he continues to grow, but right now, he's not having it! When he visits, I love playing the counting and ABC games with him, and I anxiously await as he repeats them to me. He slowly counts 1, 2, 3, 4…and when he reaches ten, he throws his hands up and we smile and clap and rejoice every time he completes a set. He tends to fill up every empty place in me. This is the kind of relationship that God desires to have with us.

Live Like You Know

The Lord told Jeremiah in chapter 1:15 "Before I formed thee in the belly I knew thee; and before thou camest forth out of the womb I sanctified thee, and I ordained thee a prophet unto the nations. God desires to fill up every empty place in us. He wants us to come to him as a child and trust Him with our lives completely. My grandson freely tests all things to see what it does or how it works. It hurts my heart to know that one day he will have to experience hurt, pain, sadness, rejection, and sin. But right now, there is not a care. At no time does he stop to question "why did this toy stopped working?" or "why can't I figure out how to work the T.V remote?" He plays with one toy at a time and if that doesn't work out, he happily moves along to the next toy! I'm so tickled that at only 2 years of age, he appears to have this all figured out! He finds what works and he moves along swiftly with no thought of what he is leaving behind. What a revelation we can get from watching a child grow and learn. Jesus tells us in Matthew 18:3 "Verily I say unto you, except ye be converted, and become as little children, ye shall not enter into the kingdom of Heaven." What was it about children did Christ want us to learn? As I watched my grandson, I can recall at one time that he was not so trusting of me until he learned who I was. I made myself always available to him and even visited as often as I could in his early weeks and months of life. This made it easy for him to trust me as the years came and went. Very much like our Heavenly Father, He is ever present with us and gives us more time than we need to learn of Him and build a lasting relationship with Him. We often become so distracted by our own situations and circumstances that our vision of Heaven becomes tainted. We'd much rather push that aside and deal with the chaos as best we know how, but don't you know that He is the answer to all of the chaos in your life? He gives us wisdom and understanding to face and overcome the madness that tends to erupt our lives without warning. When we have a relationship with the Father, our worlds could be hanging upside down, but there is a peace that will surpass all of our limited understanding. Because we trust in the Lord, we never have to fear what may arise. In the midst of the storm we can boldly say **"Lord I trust you."**

We are the complete opposite as adults. We have grown up, and from a place of innocence and trust, we have learned patterns or ways of living and handling situations from those around us that may not be the best answer to our problems. Although the remedies to overcoming obstacles has worked differently for different people, we still put so much trust in worldly resources. We have forgotten our FIRST LOVE and have sought help outside of Him. The temporary relief that has come from these worldly resources have only caused us to sink further in doubt and unbelief. When are we going to learn to just "stand" on the promises of God and not be moved by what we can physically see? My Pastor preached a message that said "Some things you just have to deal with" and he talked about how Peter did not want the Roman soldiers (when they came for Jesus) to take Him so he drew his sword and cut off the ear of one of the soldiers. But Jesus told him again to put away his sword because "If you live by the sword, you will also die by the sword," (Matthew 26:52). I received some disturbing news recently that left me feeling void on the inside like my strength was completely gone. I began to entertain thoughts of "how could God allow this to happen?" "Lord, what next?" For a moment, I thought that I would just give up. I asked myself "why am I still holding on?" I remembered God's message to me previously and immediately I was able to cast down those thoughts and move forward in faith! I repented of even allowing those thoughts to enter my mind when I know WHO is in control of all that I will ever face in life. I said "Lord, I know that this is only a distraction that the enemy has sent to turn my focus away from YOU and to this problem, but I rebuke the problem in the name of Jesus!" The enemy has you right where he wants you when he can make you lose focus of who God is to you. I began to bless the name of the Lord. See trusting God is not just something that you do when things are going well. When all hell is about to break loose in your life, I dare you to lift those hands and give God glory! Say hallelujah anyhow! The thief comes only to steal, kill, and destroy; "I have come" says the Lord, "that you might have life, and have it more abundantly" (John 10:10). Don't let the enemy rob you of your joy by pressing you with situations beyond your ability to control, but HOPE THOU IN GOD!

Why am I discouraged? Why is my heart so sad?

Teresa A. Stith

I will put my hope in God!

I will praise Him again–

my Savior and my God! (Psalm 43:5).

Prayer: Lord help us to become as children who trust in You completely. Let us not be distracted by the things in this world that is only sent to make us lose sight of the provisions that You have already made. Let Your mind be our thoughts daily as we reflect on Your goodness and mercy. Thank You that You are ever present with us, helping us and keeping us when we can't even keep ourselves. Thank You for the precious Holy Ghost who leads us and guides us on this journey and shows us things that we can't see with our natural eyes. It is a marvelous thing to be chosen by You. Help us to live daily "Like We Know" that You have given us grace, faith, and hope to believe You for greater. We love you Lord. Amen.

THE RECAP
LIVE LIKE YOU KNOW

So what did you learn about embracing your freedom in Christ and "Living Like You Know?" Let's discuss.

The first thing we learned is that "if the Son therefore shall make you free, ye shall be free indeed" (John 8:36). Jesus has clearly made us free through His redemptive work on the Cross and by the shedding of His blood for our sins. We must believe and grasp this. Knowing that we are already free and forgiven, helps us to live each day with expectancy and hope. All of our sins past, present, and future have been forgiven. However, this is not an occasion to continue in sin because we are freed from it (Romans 6: 1, 2). To stay free, we must continue to avoid going back to places and things and re-entangling ourselves with what we have been delivered from. We must choose daily to follow hard after Christ and keep His commandments if we want to meet Him in peace.

I've learned through my own Leaders that God was MORE THAN ENOUGH. I've seen this exemplified time and time again in their lives. God is an All- Sufficient God, and we must be willing to wait on Him. We did not get into our messes overnight and it will take more than one night to come out. We must be willing to endure the process which includes transformation of thoughts, behavior, and obedience to God. When God delivers you, do not feel that you ever have to return to a life of torment and sin because God is not moving fast enough for you. That's a trick of the enemy. In the process of waiting, you may have to lose some stuff, but what I have learned even while writing this book, is that the ending of one thing is surely the beginning of something else. So let life happen!

Listen, if you've been hurt by church folk, DO NOT leave the church. In Christ, we should be able to resolve issues with one another by addressing them and communicating effectively. The Spirit of God in us directs our paths and teaches us how to respond in love toward our brothers and sisters in the faith. One thing that we must remember is that we all are in need of God's grace and mercy. No one has it all together for we are all striving to arrive. The Bible says that the strong should bear the infirmities of the weak or be considerate of those who are sensitive about things like this and not to just please ourselves (Romans 15: 1). So there may be times that we have to teach people how to conduct themselves as children of God. If we are truly born of the Spirit of God, we will take heed to that instruction without anger, bitterness, or strife.

    We learned to "let go and let God." You cannot live freely trying to hold on to things in this world. God has given us freely all things to enjoy, but we should not become attached to these things. I've had to recently detach myself from something that meant a lot to me. The awesome thing about this was that God had already allowed me to make peace with the thing a whole week before it actually happened. The Spirit kept whispering that I was "dying" and I begin to study the process of dying not fully understanding what the Lord was doing. I understood though, that to live, I had to be willing to die! So I begin to detach myself from some things. Some of these things I acquired through poor planning, and hasty decisions and there is always a consequence to such things. Rather than a blessing, some things had become burdens for me, all because of the timing. Timing is everything. We learned that time and chance happens to us all, but we have to wait on our time. The Bible says "You desire but do not have, so you kill. You covet but you cannot get what you want, so you quarrel and fight. You do not have because you do not ask God. When you ask, you do not receive, because you ask with wrong motives, that you may spend what you get on your pleasures" (James 4: 2-3 NIV). God knows what our intents are. If we are honest with ourselves, we know what our intents are. God wants to bless us, and He wants us to be good stewards over what He gives us. He wants us to share what He blesses us to obtain to help others.

    We have also learned that the love of God constrains or controls us. God wants us to succeed and prosper so He has sent us a Comforter, the Holy

Ghost to lead us and guide us and teach us God's ways. He gives us the power to do what seems impossible for us and He equips us by providing Spiritual weapons that we should use daily to combat the dark forces of satan. We've learned that God has not given us the spirit of fear, but of power, love, and a sound mind (2 Tim. 1:7). Fear prevents us from moving forward in faith and faith compels us to go even when we cannot see our way. We must trust God to lead us. If the Spirit of God in us is pulling us to go, we must not be afraid to STEP. We must use good Christian sense by asking ourselves constantly, "What would Jesus do?" We do not have the answers, if we did, we would not need Christ. But because we do not, we must not trust in our abilities alone. He's the only ONE who can do exceedingly and abundantly above all that we are able to ask or think, according to the power that is at work in us (Eph. 3:20)

  And lastly, we must remember and recall what God has already said. If God is silent, it may be because He is waiting patiently for you to follow the instructions that He has already given you. He has not forgotten what He said. Our answers and our freedom rest on our willingness to obey what God has told us to do. There are many other points to ponder in this book. To embrace our freedom in Christ, we must go to God in all sincerity and ASK Him to help us to "incline our ears" to hear and receive His instructions. Much of what I've had to endure came through experience because I was hard-headed, stiff-necked, and stubborn. I've had to learn things the hard way, and I've had to suffer for much of what I have. I pray that you will not have to suffer to the extent that I have and that you will learn through and from my mistakes to prevent prolonging your stay in this place. I thank my God though, that even in my suffering, I came to know Him. I have a relationship with the Father and that to me my friends, is PRICELESS. However, if I had to go this way again, I would choose obedience over sacrifice any day.

LIVING LIFE on PURPOSE

I had absolutely no idea what awaited me on the other side of "through" but since I've been on this side, nothing can make me go back to that from whence I came. I would have never discovered what God could do with my life, had I not surrendered it all to Him. This does not mean that I won't face tough times like everyone else, but there's peace in knowing that the battle has already been won! Discovering my purpose and walking in it has been the best thing that has ever happened to me.

To date, my ministry "A Faith That Works" has reached hundreds of thousands of people around the world from many different countries, cities, states, etc. This is a ministry that I had absolutely nothing to do with, it was birthed in me through the Holy Ghost. God gets ALL the glory. I have enjoyed the places that it has taken me and all the people that it has allowed me to be connected to. Divine favor has come through obedience to the work of Jesus Christ in me. I tell you the truth, Jesus is the BEST thing that has ever happened to me. Live Like You Know, and Live Life on Purpose.

Our whole purpose in life is to do the will of Him who sent us. I don't have silver and I don't have gold, but such as I have, I give to those whom I come in contact with. The journey has been amazing.

Live Like You Know

You must be ready to go even if you have to go alone. Embracing your freedom in Christ may mean you might have to face some giants on their territory.

Remember, they that are with you, are MORE than they that are against you! (2 Kings 6: 16).

ABOUT THE AUTHOR

Teresa continues to amaze readers with her straightforwardness when it comes to the word of God. She absolutely loves planting seeds of hope in the minds and hearts of her audience believing that God has the final say in all things and that change is prominent to

Teresa A. Stith

"Living Like You Know and Embracing Freedom in Christ. She does not sugar-coat the word of God, but delivers it just like her Leaders delivered it to her...in TRUTH! This is her third published work in less than 2 years. Her other titles include "A Faith That Works, Moving From Seeing To Believing" "The Real Purpose Behind The Hat, The Broken Leading The Broken" and her upcoming titles "Writing About Writing" "A Faith That Works Devotional for men and women" "STEP, The Day I Told Myself Enough Is Enough", "Advancing the Kingdom of God" and "What Has It Cost You To Die?" She writes from a Spiritual genre and targets those individuals whose been broken-hearted, physically and sexually abused, those involved in domestic violence or abusive relationships, those emotionally scarred, having suicidal thoughts, etc. She is a lifter-upper of your head. She motivates, encourages, and build you up in the area of your faith, so that you can withstand and endure in this last hour. She has a strong love and compassion for people and is ADORED by MILLIONS! Visit her website at afaiththatworks.com or email at afaiththatworks@outlook.com. You can also visit her Facebook Fan Page at 'Afaiththatworks. Visit her online store at:

https://faith-it-to-make-it.myshopify.com and last but certainly not least, find all her books here:

https://amazon.com/author/teresastith

Thank you so earnestly for all of your love, prayers, and support. May God richly bless each of you.

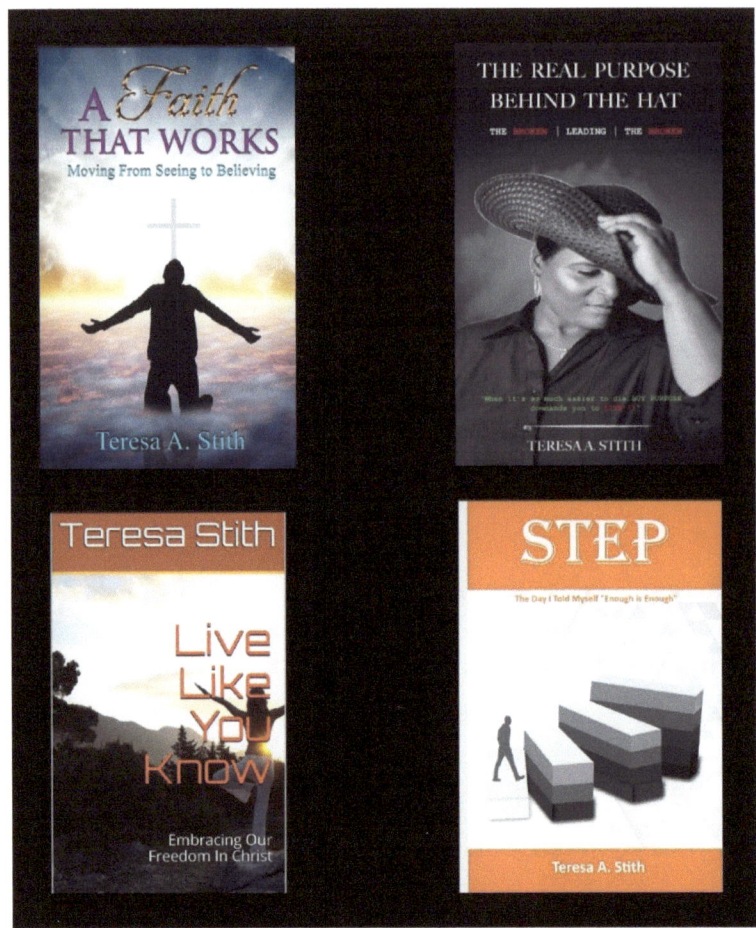

Upcoming Titles:

Advancing the Kingdom of God
Writing About Writing
What Has It Cost You To Die?
A Faith That Works Devotional For Men/ Women
The Faith Angel- Children's Book

www.ingramcontent.com/pod-product-compliance
Lightning Source LLC
Chambersburg PA
CBHW041642090426
42736CB00034BA/6